New York in Four Seasons

MICHAEL STORRINGS

Author of *A Very New York Christmas*

WITH A FOREWORD BY KRISTIN CHENOWETH

St. Martin's Press ☙ New York

CHRISTMAS

NEW YEAR'S
EVE

CHINESE
NEW YEAR

FALL

WINTER

HANNUKAH

LABOR DAY
WEEKEND

VILLAGE
HALLOWEEN
PARADE

THANKSGIVING
DAY PARADE

MUSEUM MILE
FESTIVAL

FOURTH OF
JULY

SPRING

SUMMER

MERMAID
PARADE

ST. PATRICK'S
DAY PARADE

OPENING DAY
BASEBALL

MEMORIAL
DAY

NEW YORK THROUGH THE SEASONS

TABLE OF CONTENTS

FALL

SEPTEMBER, OCTOBER, NOVEMBER

WINTER

DECEMBER, JANUARY, FEBRUARY

SPRING
MARCH, APRIL, MAY

SUMMER
JUNE, JULY, AUGUST

FOREWORD

Nowhere else in the world can you simultaneously feel the exhilarating pulse of a vibrant city and also have at your disposal the serenity of an oasis like Central Park. During the summer, I often take my dog, Madeline Kahn Chenoweth, out to the park for a walk. When the weather is just right, we escape the hustle and bustle of the city and head toward the Mall on the east side of the park, and walk beneath the beautiful trees that hang down each side of the path—a scene just like the one Michael has so beautifully captured in this book. See, I grew up in Oklahoma, where enjoying the outdoors was as natural as breathing, so I savor any opportunity I get to go out and grab a breath of fresh air (and a bit of exercise).

But there's nothing better than walking out of Central Park and on to Fifth Avenue, where I can continue to stretch my legs and engage in one of my favorite indoor activities: shopping. My favorite time of the year to do this is winter, when all of the window displays are set up for the holidays. One of the most exciting window displays is at Saks Fifth Avenue. They always seem to create a story with their designs, and I feel like I could stare at those windows forever and get lost in their magic.

My absolutely favorite thing about New York in *any* season, though, is the fact that no matter where I go, music is constantly in the air. From the concerts and performers in Central Park to the carolers who sing outside stores and down the streets during the holidays, New York fills my heart with the sound of music... and I wouldn't have it any other way.

KRISTIN CHENOWETH

INTRODUCTION

Psst… I have a secret! I am in love with New York. I mean really over the moon: tongue-tying, heart-pounding, butterflies-in-stomach feeling, can't get enough of—I think of the city as My Love.

This makes me the luckiest guy, because every day I wake up in love.

I dote on New York's colors, people, buildings, textures, sounds, and whatever else My Love offers. I just want to draw it. Sideways, backward, inside out, zigzaggy, constantly!

This Love of mine never gets boring. With each season, the city presents me with different things that perpetually make me a helpless admirer.

In autumn, its complexion of tangerine and honey radiates on trees and clothes; the coolness of its breath sets the tone for the Halloween Parade and the New York City Marathon. When it snows, the whiteness of its newly adorned winter garment becomes the backdrop for the explosion of red, green, blue, and silver of Christmas and Hanukkah celebrations, and the gold and red of the Chinese New Year.

Then the warmth of spring arrives, enabling me to venture onto its streets, to walk under blossoming trees and wear sherbet pastels for Easter and other rites of the season.

And the freedom it offers in summer, when I lie out under its bright cyan skies or listen to music in a vast green oasis, watching a multitude of colors radiating in its sky…

My Love is pure joy!

This book is my testament to my city—My Love. I hope that you will enjoy perusing my paintings, and that you discover for yourself some new favorite places and events that My Love has to offer.

Perhaps you'll even fall as deeply in love as I have!

MICHAEL STORRINGS

FALL

SEPTEMBER, OCTOBER, NOVEMBER

"DON'T YOU LOVE NEW YORK IN THE FALL. IT MAKES ME WANT TO BUY SCHOOL SUPPLIES.
I WOULD SEND YOU A BOUQUET OF NEWLY SHARPENED PENCILS
IF I KNEW YOUR NAME AND ADDRESS." — NORA EPHRON

LABOR DAY WEEKEND

Labor Day weekend in and around the city is a heady celebration of the last days of summer, when New Yorkers enjoy one last sandy beach day or rooftop cocktail, bid farewell to summer cottages, and prepare for the adrenaline rush of reentry to work and school. Picnickers flock to Central Park, Riverside Park, Prospect Park, and the city's seventeen hundred other parks to milk the last hours of summer's leisurely pace. The weekend reaches a crescendo with the colorful costumes and street dancing of the West Indian Day Parade on Brooklyn's Eastern Parkway.

ROOFTOP PARTY, BROOKLYN

CHILE PEPPER FESTIVAL

Each October, purveyors of exotic and fiery chiles, a selection of fine chocolatiers, a wide variety of artisanal food makers, and an array of red-hot bands turn the Brooklyn Botanic Garden into a food-and-music-lover's paradise.

FEAST OF SAN GENNARO

Dedicated to the patron saint of Naples, the Feast of San Gennaro was first held in Little Italy in 1926. Today, food stands, processions, music performances, rides, and arcade games bring a carnivalesque atmosphere— and more than a million visitors—to the neighborhood's narrow streets for eleven days in September.

ONE WORLD TRADE CENTER AND LOWER MANHATTAN

Lower Manhattan has undergone multiple transformations during its four hundred-year-old history: from Dutch colonial outpost to bustling port city to financial center of the world to site of the World Trade Center and the attacks of September 11, 2001. Today, this unique swath of the city is a vibrant hub of culture and commerce—all the more so in autumn, when Wall Street revs up after summer vacations and thousands gather at the National September 11 Memorial & Museum for tributes marking the anniversary of 9/11. The Memorial's twin reflecting pools and serene, tree-shaded plaza border the One World Trade Center skyscraper rising at the northwest corner of the former Twin Towers site. Each September 11, two beacons of light symbolizing the fallen towers are projected from Ground Zero into the sky, a moving remembrance

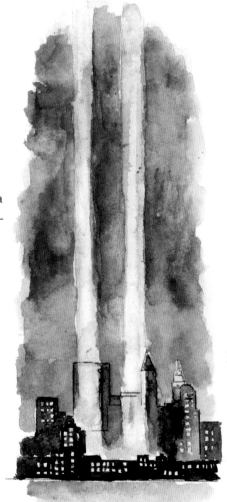

BEACONS OF LIGHT FOR
WORLD TRADE CENTER TRIBUTE

visible from miles around. In October, autumn leaves on hundreds of oak trees surrounding the reflecting pools turn the plaza into a brilliant canvas of deep golds, reds, and pinks. The Indian summer days of early autumn reflect lower Manhattan and New York Harbor at its best: sunlight sparkling on the water, the Statue of Liberty in clear view, ferries chugging to and from Ellis Island and the Staten Island ferry terminal, and municipal workers scurrying past public sculpture on their way to city hall. The area's monuments are many, including the old US Custom House (now the National Museum of the American Indian) and the Woolworth Building. On a typical warm day, tourists and stockbrokers, attorneys and schoolchildren might be enjoying an alfresco lunch in Battery Park or a lunchtime concert in historic Trinity Church at the head of Wall Street.

BROADWAY AND OPERA SEASON OPENINGS

September signals the start of "the season," when New York's opera and theater companies debut new productions, and elegant red-carpet opening galas are a must for the city's social set and power brokers. Opening night as a social tradition began in the late nineteenth century among New York's "Knickerbockers," the blue blood families who founded the first Metropolitan Opera House in 1883 at Broadway and 39th Street. These days, the Monday-night opening galas at Lincoln Center begin with a parade of opera stars and celebrities arriving at dusk in black tie and shimmering gowns.

METROPOLITAN OPERA, LINCOLN CENTER

THE GYPSY ROBE

On Broadway, one beloved behind-the-scenes opening-night ritual is the Gypsy Robe. Each time a new musical opens, a decorated dressing gown is presented to the chorus member with the most Broadway credits. In the quiet theater, before the audience arrives, the cast forms a circle on the stage and the robe is bestowed on the lucky cast member—the "gypsy." Each new gypsy adds his or her own theater memorabilia to the robe, and when the robe is full, it is retired.

"New York is definitely haunted. Old lovers, ex-boyfriends, anyone you have unresolved issues with you are bound to run into again and again until you resolve them."

—Sarah Jessica Parker, as Carrie Bradshaw in *Sex and the City*

THE VILLAGE HALLOWEEN PARADE

THE EMPIRE STATE
BUILDING DRESSED UP
FOR HALLOWEEN

America's largest night parade gets underway each October 31 in the heart of Greenwich Village, when thousands of costumed revelers, street performers, and giant puppets promenade up Sixth Avenue in the Village Halloween parade. The pageant has been called the "largest street party in the world," drawing more than fifty thousand participants and two million spectators to an annual ritual that celebrates the city's diversity and creative energy. A highlight of the event is more than fifty elaborate, articulated puppets—skeletons and fantastical creatures floating above the crowd—a fixture of the parade since its founding in 1974 by puppeteer and mask maker Ralph Lee. A ten-foot spider puppet traditionally appears to "bless" the event by crawling up and down the tower of the Gothic-style Jefferson Market Library at the corner of Tenth Street.

Anyone in costume is welcome to join the parade, and in keeping with the Village's tradition of tolerance, you'll see not only witches and ghouls but also plenty of celebrity satirists, fairy tale cross-dressers, and brilliant body paint worthy of an artist's studio, in addition to more than fifty bands and plenty of dancing. The parade was named "a true cultural treasure" by mayoral proclamation in 1994 and remains a safe and beloved annual event.

US OPEN

The United States Open Tennis Championship, held annually in late August and early September, is an exciting harbinger of autumn in New York. The world's best tennis players and fans from across the globe converge at the USTA Billie Jean King National Tennis Center in Queens for two weeks in the fourth and final grand slam event of the year.

NEW YORK CITY MARATHON

From its beginnings in 1970, when 127 people ran the first city marathon in Central Park (only 55 finished!), the New York City Marathon has grown to be the world's largest. Each year on the first Sunday in November, nearly 50,000 runners gather in the predawn hours on Staten Island for the start of the 26.2-mile race, which winds through all five boroughs and across five city bridges before ending amid cheering crowds in Central Park.

FASHION WEEK

First held in 1943 exclusively for the fashion press, Fashion Week in New York is now among the city's largest—and certainly most glamorous—media events. Twice each year, more than eighty international designers showcase their collections to one hundred thousand industry insiders, celebrities, hangers-on, and the fashion obsessed from around the world.

BLESSING OF THE ANIMALS

Early autumn brings the Feast of St. Francis of Assisi and the Blessing of the Animals at the Cathedral of St. John the Divine, St. Bart's, and Catholic churches throughout the city. Visitors bring cats,

dogs, tortoises, camels, elephants, and all manner of creatures to be blessed by a member of the clergy in the name of St. Francis, a lover and champion of animals and nature.

ROSH HASHANAH

Rosh Hashanah, the Jewish New Year, is the first of the High Holy Days—the most important days of the Jewish calendar. Observant Jews blow the shofar (a ram's horn) in celebration and eat foods such as apples and honey to symbolize the sweetness of the New Year.

Many Jewish people in New York can be found near one of the rivers, where they recite prayers and perform the ritual of *tashlikh*, the throwing of pieces of bread or small stones into the water, symbolically casting away their sins. *L'shanah tovah!* (For a good year!)

THANKSGIVING EVE BALLOON VIEWING

The first Macy's Thanksgiving Day Parade was held in 1924, when animals from the Central Park Zoo were a featured attraction along with floats and musical bands. In the early days, balloons outfitted with return address labels were released into the air at the end of the parade. The lucky people who found and returned the balloons received a special gift from Macy's.

Today, thousands visit Central Park West and Seventy-seventh Street on Thanksgiving eve to view the hundred or so balloons being inflated.

With the beautiful American Museum of Natural History in the background, you can watch as balloon technicians and their helpers go about the business of bringing Snoopy, Mickey Mouse, Kermit the Frog, SpongeBob SquarePants, Kung Fu Panda, and dozens of other characters into gravity-defying, three-dimensional life. Rope netting keeps the characters in place until they begin their journey downtown to Thirty-fourth Street at 9:00 a.m. on Thanksgiving morning!

WINTER

December, January, February

"I was raised in California, so this whole New York winter thing is completely new for me. I've already justified buying seven coats." —Blake Lively

CHRISTMAS IN NEW YORK CITY

At Christmastime, the entire city seems to dress up in variations of green and red, silver glitter and white snow, bringing a magical luster to many of the city's most beloved neighborhoods and landmarks.

The Empire State Building sets the tone from on high with dazzling displays of Christmas colors. Stroll up Fifth Avenue to Bryant Park, where you will find a Winter Holiday Village in which you can both ice-skate and shop!

Herald angels brighten the plaza and ice-skaters twirl and spill on the ice at nearby Rockefeller Center, while across Sixth Avenue, visitors flock to Radio City Music Hall to see the Christmas Spectacular featuring the Rockettes. Across town, Grand Central Terminal hosts a sensational laser light show that's repeated throughout the day in its main concourse, and bustles with a colorful Holiday Fair in Vanderbilt Hall.

Farther uptown, the Plaza Hotel, which anchors the southeast corner of Central Park, has a beautiful Christmas tree in its entrance hall, the lighting of which is a highlight of the hotel's calendar. This is an excellent starting point for a stroll up through Central Park, where you can stop and watch the animals at the Central Park Zoo open their Christmas presents.

Washington Square Park, the recently restored gem at the heart of Greenwich Village, is the site of a fittingly bohemian tree lighting featuring music and caroling—beautifully framed by Washington Square Arch.

In Brooklyn, there is no greater homegrown exhibition of Christmas spirit than the over-the-top building decorations in Dyker Heights, where home owners employ dioramas, larger-than-life figures, crèches, and tens of thousands of lights. As one observer remarked, "It's almost as though Christmas just decided to explode in the middle of Brooklyn!"

Get a taste of an elegant nineteenth-century Bronx Christmas at the Bartow-Pell Mansion, a Federal-style National Historic Landmark. Here you can take a candle-light tour of the interior, serenaded by carolers dressed in Victorian garb.

The Holiday Train Show at the New York Botanical Garden, in which model trains chug past New York landmarks constructed entirely of twigs, bark, branches, and other plant material, is not to be missed.

And of course, don't forget to visit the "real" Santas at Macy's and uptown at the Plaza Hotel!

LINCOLN CENTER

THE NUTCRACKER

The story of Drosselmeyer's magical Nutcracker, saved from the Mouse King by the innocent Clara—in a dream world populated by Sugar Plum Fairies, Chinese Tea dancers, and Russian Candy Cane dancers—is an irresistible staple of Christmas in New York. The glittering production staged by the New York City Ballet is without doubt the crown jewel, but among the many worthy others, the Joffrey Ballet School and the *Yorkville Nutcracker* productions both feature young, up-and-coming local dancers!

HANUKKAH IN NEW YORK

Hanukkah is big in New York—literally: the "world's largest menorah" (approximately thirty-two feet tall) can be found in Grand Army Plaza in Brooklyn, rivaled closely by a four thousand-pound structure placed near the southeast corner of Central Park.

Called the festival of lights, Hanukkah's chief ritual centers on the lighting of the eight candles of the menorah, adding one each night for eight successive nights (the ninth branch of the menorah holds the *shamash*, or the candle that is used to light all the others). In homes and synagogues throughout the five boroughs, candles are lit from right to left, the direction in which Hebrew is read, while prayers are recited.

Hanukkah is celebrated with the eating of *latkes* (potato pancakes), *bimuelos* (fritters), and *sufganiyot* (round jelly doughnuts) and the singing of songs. Children play with *dreidels*, four-sided tops, trading *gelt* (Hanukkah "money" that is actually chocolate wrapped in gold foil).

THE WORLD'S LARGEST MENORAH IS LIT FROM A CHERRY PICKER.

THE "ANGEL TREE"

In December, chamber music and other seasonal sounds echo in the Medieval Sculpture Hall at the Metropolitan Museum of Art, where the museum's famed "angel tree" stands each Christmas. The tree, adorned with candles and beautiful eighteenth-century Neapolitan angel figurines, is the centerpiece of a wonderfully Baroque, lifelike nativity scene. The Neapolitan figurines were donated to the museum in 1964 by the artist and collector Loretta Hines Howard.

ORIGAMI TREE

ORGANIZERS SELECT A DIFFERENT THEME FOR THE TREE EACH YEAR.

For more than forty years, the American Museum of Natural History has marked the start of the holiday season by unveiling its beautiful origami tree, decorated with more than five hundred brightly colored, hand-folded paper snakes, frogs, spiders, dinosaurs, butterflies, whales, and spaceships created by origami artists from all over the world.

DICKENS AT THE MORGAN LIBRARY

The beautiful Morgan Library & Museum owns one of the original manuscripts of Charles Dickens' *A Christmas Carol*, and this is the catalyst for a day of fun and revelry hosted by the Morgan each December. Kids will be entertained throughout the day by puppets, art activities, and costumed characters strolling and singing. The day is highlighted by a dramatic reading of *A Christmas Carol* (stay out of Scrooge's way!) held right in front of the fireplace and among the gilded stacks of Mr. Morgan's inner sanctum. The Morgan, once the private mansion of the financier J. P. Morgan—a renowned collector of art, books, and artifacts of all kinds—is now a magnificent window to New York in the Gilded Age.

AVERY FISHER HALL

HANDEL'S MESSIAH AT LINCOLN CENTER

George Frideric Handel's beloved English-language oratorio is performed all over the city each December by a wide variety of choral groups. Among the most popular: the New York Philharmonic; the Oratorio Society of New York; and the Masterwork Chorus. A joyful sing-along *Messiah* has been performed at the Judson Memorial Church in Greenwich Village each year for more than thirty years!

CHRISTMAS EVE MIDNIGHT MASS, ST. PATRICK'S CATHEDRAL

More than three thousand worshippers gather under the soaring vaults of St. Patrick's Cathedral on Fifth Avenue each Christmas eve for a standing-room-only midnight Mass that draws tourists, citizens, and VIPs like the mayor. Entering the cathedral through heavy bronze doors, visitors leave the clamor and festivities of midtown behind to enter a magical space. Inside the Gothic Revival–style cathedral, crimson poinsettias, wreaths, and dozens of garlands decorate the altar and massive columns, and glimmering lights illuminate stained glass windows. The cathedral boasts a nearly life-size nativity scene with delicate wooden figures carved in Italy (in 2011, a dog modeled after the rector's Labrador retriever was added to the crèche). Two historic organs and choirs fill the interior with traditional Christmas music.

Christmas has been celebrated at St. Patrick's for more than 130 years, since the cathedral's dedication in 1879, twenty years after the first cornerstone was laid in 1858. The service was televised nationally for the first time in 1948. Today, preparations for Christmas Eve Mass begin in the summer, and admission is by ticket only.

NEW YEAR'S EVE IN NEW YORK

New Yorkers go all-out on New Year's Eve, dressing for the occasion and flocking to special events at nightclubs, restaurants, and private parties.

A million people (give or take) descend on Times Square to watch the fabled ball drop from a flagpole atop One Times Square, and nearly a billion watch the event live on television, making those few blocks of midtown feel as though they really are the center of the universe. Jaw-dropping neon billboards flash as singers and performers entertain the crowd, and confetti and joyous shouts fill the air in anticipation of the countdown to 11:59 p.m., when the ball begins its sixty-second descent to the base of the specially designed flagpole, signifying the New Year when it reaches the bottom.

Cleanup crews spring into action nearly the moment the ball drops, sweeping up the estimated fifty tons of confetti, hats, balloons, pizza boxes, and empty soda bottles left behind by revelers. By midmorning, you would never know the area had just hosted the world's largest party.

Around lunchtime on New Year's Day, hundreds of members of the Coney Island Polar Bear Club and guest swimmers conquer their fears, not to mention common sense, by plunging into the frigid waters of the Atlantic. That's been a New York tradition since 1903!

POLAR BEAR CLUB NEW YEAR'S
DAY SWIM AT CONEY ISLAND

鼠
RAT

牛
OX

虎
TIGER

兔
RABBIT

龍
DRAGON

蛇
SNAKE

CHINESE NEW YEAR

Larger-than-life, lavishly colored, wildly ornate dragons and lions dance acrobatically through the streets of Chinatown in downtown Manhattan each year during the Chinatown Lunar New Year Parade & Festival in celebration of the lunar New Year, which falls in January or February of the Western calendar.

40

The narrow thoroughfares of Chinatown teem with magnificently decorated floats, acrobats, magicians, and more than five thousand performers, as a cacophony of lutes, gongs, and marching bands fills the air. The pops of firecrackers keep evil spirits at bay, while generous swashes of red and gold, the auspicious colors of good health and good fortune, bring revelers happy tidings for the New Year.

Food vendors and neighborhood restaurants offer an array of dumplings and a host of other Chinese delicacies, many with the words "good fortune" added to the name for the occasion. The animal symbols of the Chinese zodiac abound, as the attributes of each animal combine and interact to shape the destiny of the coming year.

馬 HORSE

羊 GOAT

猴 MONKEY

雞 ROOSTER

狗 DOG

豬 PIG

41

WESTMINSTER DOG SHOW

The Westminster Kennel Club Dog Show has been a tradition in New York since 1877, making it the second-oldest continuously running sporting event in the United States, after the Kentucky Derby. Now held in Madison Square Garden over two days in February, the show is limited to 3,200 canine competitors of virtually every breed recognized by the American Kennel Club. Breeds are organized into groups: sporting, hound, working, terrier, toy, nonsporting, and herding; the dogs compete for best in breed, then best in group, and finally, the most coveted prize, best in show.

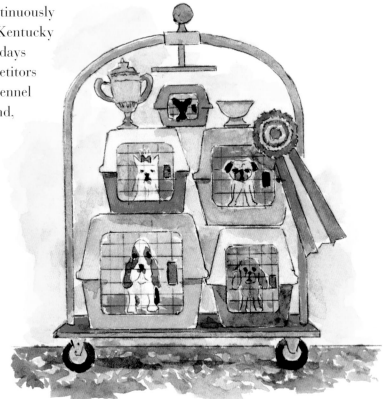

Westminster gets its name from a long-gone hotel in Manhattan, where "sporting gentlemen" (i.e., hunters) would gather in the bar. Eventually they formed a club and bought a training area and kennel—and in the spirit of camaraderie, named it after their favorite drinking haunt.

ROOM SERVICE, PLEASE.
DOGS AND THEIR OWNERS CAN BE FOUND IN
MANY OF THE CITY'S FINEST HOTELS.

CENTRAL PAR

SPRING
MARCH, APRIL, MAY

"I STUCK MY HEAD OUT THE WINDOW THIS MORNING
AND SPRING KISSED ME BANG IN THE FACE."
—LANGSTON HUGHES

ST. PATRICK'S DAY PARADE

New York City's St. Patrick's Day Parade is one-of-a-kind event—an amalgam of Irish pride, local politics, religious ritual, and no-holds-barred partying. 150,000-plus marchers—high school bands, bagpipe players, police, firefighters, the thirty-two Irish county societies, military groups, and (of course) politicians—gather at Fifth Avenue and Forty-fourth Street for the 1.5-mile march past St. Patrick's Cathedral to the American Irish Historical Society at Seventy-ninth Street. Spectators number in the millions. First held in 1762, it is the largest St. Patrick's Day Parade in the world, and one of the oldest. Erin go bragh!

VIEWING PLATFORM
FOR THE CARDINAL

FIFTH AVE

NYPD

FLOWER DISPLAYS

Come late March, New Yorkers are all too ready to banish winter's gray chill with citywide floral extravaganzas. In midtown, the annual Macy's Flower Show transforms the historic Herald Square store into a lush oasis of bouquets, topiaries, and blossom canopies; Rockefeller Plaza, to the north, is bursting with tulips. In the Bronx, the Orchid Show at The New York Botanical Garden showcases thousands of exotic species, while Daffodil Hill in the Brooklyn Botanic Garden blooms yellow and buds start to pop in the Cranford Rose Garden, peaking in June. The Queens Botanical Garden, with its Herb, Bee, and Victorian-style Wedding Gardens, has its origins in the 1939 World's Fair.

CENTRAL PARK

FIFTH AVE

BROOKLYN

BRONX

QUEENS

BASEBALL OPENING DAY

In New York, one of spring's most highly anticipated events is the Subway Series—baseball games played between New York's two home teams, the Mets and the Yankees. Both teams' stadiums are easily accessible via the city's subway system:

THE BRONX IS HOME TO YANKEE STADIUM.

Yankee Stadium in the Bronx via the 4 or D train; Citi Field (the Mets' home in Queens) via the 7 train. The two teams met in the 2000 World Series, won by the Yankees, four games to one. See if you can spot the players wearing retired numbers!

CITI FIELD, THE METS' HOME, IS IN QUEENS.

EASTER PARADE ON FIFTH AVENUE

On Easter Sunday, New Yorkers by the thousands exchange their de rigueur winter black for pastel and multicolored finery and promenade along Fifth Avenue at the annual Easter Parade and Bonnet Festival. Children, out-of-towners, and even pets are all welcome at this beloved spring spectacle, where the fun is in spotting all manner of lavish folded, sculpted, and flower-adorned hats—the larger the better!

The tradition began in the mid-nineteenth century, when the city's social elite would attend Easter church services and then parade their finery on Fifth Avenue, the most prestigious thoroughfare in the city. Today, the avenue is closed to traffic between Forty-ninth and Fifty-seventh streets from 10:00 a.m. to about 4:00 p.m. on the day of the parade, and you're just as likely to see families dressed in genteel vintage finery—lace, top hats, and furs— as you are beat box-toting hip-hop Easter bunnies in dazzling neon colors.

EASTER EGG HUNT ON THE GREAT HILL IN CENTRAL PARK

CHERRY BLOSSOM FESTIVAL

The Brooklyn Botanic Garden's (BBG's) annual *Sakura Matsuri*, (Japanese for "Cherry Blossom Festival"), takes place over two weekend days, usually in April, and draws thousands of people from all over the world. The garden's Cherry Esplanade comes alive with kimonos, Japanese anime characters, and camera-toting fans determined to capture the glorious pink blossoms of *Prunus* 'Kanzan' at the height of their perfection. *Taiko* drumming and other music and dance, food, and demonstrations of Japanese culture are all part of the celebration. For die-hard blossom fans, an interactive "CherryWatch" map on the BBG Web site allows you to monitor the trees' status as the season progresses.

SNUG HARBOR CULTURAL CENTER

SNUG HARBOR ALLÉE

PAGODA BUILDING AND THE WEISS GLASS GAZEBO

Built as a home for retired sailors, Snug Harbor is now a beautiful and relaxing eighty-three-acre city park that is dotted with twenty-six landmarked nineteenth-century buildings. Set along the northern shore of Staten Island along the Kill van Kull, Snug Harbor is also home to the Staten Island Botanical Garden, whose highlights include the White Garden (modeled on Vita Sackville-West's Sissinghurst); Connie Gretz's Secret Garden, inspired by the garden in the Frances Hodgson Burnett's eponymous classic children's novel; the Chinese Scholar's Garden, with eight pavilions, a koi pond, and dramatic rock formations; and the Allée, a tunnel-arch of 120 upright hornbeams.

THE SECRET GARDEN

PARK AVENUE TULIPS

Chosen by the city in 1959 to plant the median strip along Park Avenue above the train tracks leading north from Grand Central Terminal, the Dutch immigrant and landscaper Peter van De Wetering, joined in recent years by his son, Anton, has been planting and maintaining that prized ribbon of real estate ever since. Operated since 1980 by the Fund for Park Avenue, the spring median plantings of eighty thousand tulips have expanded to include cherry trees, begonias in summer, hawthorn trees in fall, and fir trees festooned with lights in winter—bringing color and light to Park Avenue the year round.

COMMERCE STREET

GREENWICH VILLAGE WALKING TOURS

You know you're arrived in Greenwich Village when you can see the Victorian Gothic clock tower of the Jefferson Market Library, a branch of the New York Public Library since 1967, but originally designed by Frederick Clarke Withers and Calvert Vaux (of Central Park fame) as a courthouse.

BLEECKER ST.

But the beating heart of the Village is Washington Square Park, with its triumphal arch, erected in 1892. The park became famous as a hangout for beatniks and folksingers in the 1960s and remains a magnet for street performers as well as casual strollers, chess players, and neighborhood workers on their lunch hours.

West of Washington Square is Christopher Park and Stonewall, the watering hole that became the epicenter of the gay rights movement. Meander the Village's tree-lined, picturesque streets. Loop past the Cherry Lane Theater on tiny Commerce Street. Squint and you can picture these streets as they looked in the nineteenth century. Then stop in for a rest and a cupcake at the Magnolia Bakery!

CHRISTOPHER PARK
ACROSS FROM
STONEWALL INN

SOHO WALKING TOURS

Soho (for "South of Houston Street"), once an industrial neighborhood, is today one of the most chic areas in New York City, home to trendy retailers, restaurants, and hotels. Soho was homesteaded by artists in the late 1960s and 1970s, who were drawn by the magnificent cast iron buildings and their large loft spaces. Many artists frequented Vesuvio Bakery, which opened in 1920 and whose Prince Street storefront has been preserved by its current occupant, also a bakery.

The Puck Building, an office, retail, and special events building a few blocks to the east, and presided over by a gold-colored statue of the impish Puck, was once home to the humor magazine that bore the same name (*Puck* ceased publication in 1918). Old St. Patrick's Cathedral, a Gothic Revival landmark located just to the east, was the seat of the Archdiocese of New York until the current St. Patrick's Cathedral opened its doors in 1879.

PUCK

PRINCE ST.

SINGER BUILDING

OLD ST. PATRICK'S CATHEDRAL

CENTRAL PARK ZOO

Cuddly baby lambs and canopies of delicate, yellow-green leaves signal the arrival of spring at the Central Park Zoo—the perfect season to discover the zoo's more than 150 species of animals awakening from their winter slumber. Favorites include the seals and sea lions, four species of penguins in the Polar Seabirds exhibit, and the highly endangered snow leopards.

KIDS CAN POSE BEHIND THE ZOO'S FAMOUS RABBIT SCULPTURES.

New Yorkers and visitors alike adore the Delacorte Musical Clock, which spans the walkway near the Tisch Children's Zoo. It features a tambourine-playing bear, a panpipe-playing goat, and other fanciful bronze animals who dance to nursery rhymes as the clock strikes every hour and half hour. From March 21 to June 21, favorite spring tunes like "Easter Parade" and "April in Paris" accompany the dancing animals.

TRIBECA FILM FESTIVAL

Since its inception in 2002, the Tribeca Film Festival has drawn more than four million filmgoers from across the globe to movie theaters and screening rooms all over Manhattan, anchored by the festival's headquarters on Canal Street on the northern edge of Tribeca (the "Triangle Below Canal Street"). Through the years, the festival has screened more than fourteen hundred films from eighty countries.

The festival's dual goals are to expose deserving films and filmmakers to the widest possible audience and to promote New York City as a major filmmaking center. Indeed, the festival played an important role in revitalizing the image, if not the economy, of post-9/11 New York.

The festival combines Hollywood and New York City star power, major Hollywood screenings, and interesting independent, foreign, and even experimental films, bringing a heady, creative buzz to the city when the festival is on—and giving wide exposure to filmmakers who are not yet household names.

THE FESTIVAL WAS FOUNDED BY TRIBECA RESIDENT ROBERT DE NIRO WITH JANE ROSENTHAL AND CRAIG HATKOFF.

MEMORIAL DAY

Each year, the week leading up to Memorial Day weekend brings thousands of US Navy sailors, Marines, and Coast Guardsmen to the docks and streets of the New York for Fleet Week. Sea-weary sailors take in the sights and pleasures of the city. New Yorkers who haven't fled for the beach watch the parade of ships in the harbor, tug-of-war, and other contests— and even tour some of the docked vessels.

MEMORIAL DAY PARADE, DOUGLASTON, QUEENS

SUMMER
June, July, August

"I love New York on summer afternoons when every one's away.
There's something very sensuous about it—overripe, as if all sorts
of funny fruits were going to fall into your hands."
— F. Scott Fitzgerald, *The Great Gatsby*

THE MUSEUM MILE FESTIVAL

For one evening each June, the Museum Mile Festival turns upper Fifth Avenue into "New York's biggest block party," as nine of the city's major cultural institutions close the streets, open their doors, and welcome visitors from around the city and the globe.

While the entire stretch of Fifth Avenue between 82nd and 105th Streets is closed to traffic, turning it into a stroller's paradise, the nine participating museums admit visitors free of charge, offering art-related activities for kids, music, and food. Street performers and face painters add to the air of festivity, while kids with sidewalk chalk create their own en plein air masterpieces.

KIDS WITH SIDEWALK CHALK
TURN FIFTH AVENUE INTO
A GIANT CANVAS.

PARTICIPATING MUSEUMS

- *The Jewish Museum*
- *El Museo del Barrio*
- *The Neue Galerie New York*
- *The Museum for African Art*
- *The Metropolitan Museum of Art*
- *The Museum of the City of New York*
- *The Solomon R. Guggenheim Museum*
- *The National Academy Museum and School*
- *The Cooper-Hewitt, National Design Museum, Smithsonian Institution*

CONEY ISLAND

A carnivalesque atmosphere pervades Coney Island in the summer. The beach is packed with sunbathers, while fishermen try their luck from the pier. People from every walk of life stroll the boardwalk.

Thrill seekers line up for classic rides like Deno's Wonder Wheel and the Cyclone, which dominate the skyline, and the new (as of 2012) Luna Park offers rides that are rated by thrill level, from mild to extreme. Others fill the arcades, ramming each other with bumper cars, or amassing tickets to win prizes playing pinball and dozens of other games.

People line up for hotdogs at Nathan's Famous, a chain that has its origins in a single hotdog stand opened in Coney Island in 1916 by Nathan Handwerker, a Polish immigrant. Nathan's sponsors an annual hotdog-eating contest every July 4, a competitive eating event that draws an estimated forty thousand spectators and another million television viewers.

Each June since 1983, the Mermaid Parade—"the largest art parade in the nation," according to organizers—has marked the beginning of the summer season. The parade's estimated fifteen hundred participants design outlandish (and risqué!) costumes and floats that are generally centered on mermaids, sea gods, and the most exotic aquatic life you've ever seen.

THE HIGH LINE

In 2009, the High Line, a once-derelict, abandoned elevated railway on Manhattan's lower west side, reopened to the public as a state-of-the-art public park and greenway—described by a prominent architecture critic as equal parts promenade, town square, and botanical garden. Originally built as a door-to-door rail link from Penn Station to the meatpacking houses and other businesses of the area, the twenty-five-foot-high elevated line was painstakingly retrofitted as a beautifully landscaped, diversion-filled pathway that snakes through gritty industrial buildings and century-old urban infrastructure as well as gleaming new hotels, condominiums, art galleries, and boutiques.

In the words of one of its principal designers, the High Line is a "meandering ribbon with special episodes." Among the "episodes" are built-in, wooden chaise lounges mounted on the still-present rail tracks —highly sought after, especially as the sun sets over the Hudson River to the west. An outdoor amphitheater whose stage consists of four gigantic windows that frame the uptown traffic and pedestrians on Tenth Avenue gives new and literal meaning to the term *street theater*. Food vendors and artisans sell their wares in covered parts of the High Line, while colorful mosaics and art installations bring constant variety to the delightful experience of walking this urban trail.

CHAISE LOUNGES ON
RAIL TRACKS

BRONX ZOO AND NEW YORK AQUARIUM

What better way to celebrate summer than to commune with wild animals—safely, and in beautiful surroundings?

The Bronx Zoo seems to come alive in the warmer weather, especially the animals in the Congo Gorilla Forest and on the African Plains—and the Wild Asia Monorail runs only in the warm weather months.

The New York Aquarium, sited at the ocean's edge in south Brooklyn, is a great place to watch aquatic animals in action, learn about conservation, take in a show at the Aquatheater, and soak in the sun and surf.

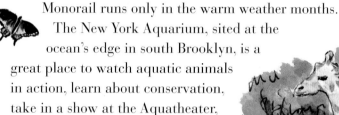

THE MONORAIL

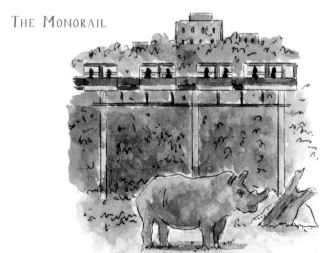

LOOKING AT A GIRAFFE AND OSTRICH ON THE AFRICAN PLAINS

FOURTH OF JULY

New Yorkers celebrate Independence Day with characteristic enthusiasm, hosting America's largest and most spectacular Independence Day fireworks display. Festivities begin just after dark, when forty thousand rockets launched from several barges send ear-popping, kaleidoscopic bursts of color over the skyline, reflected on the waters of the harbor and accompanied by music from a wide variety of artists. Hundreds of thousands of spectators line parks, streets, rooftops, and terraces bordering the rivers, or watch from Circle Line cruises and private boats in the harbor.

The pyrotechnics cap a day filled with other Fourth of July traditions: the famous Nathan's hotdog-eating contest in Coney Island, picnics in city parks, softball games, and neighborhood parades complete with Uncle Sam hats and plenty of red, white, and blue.

✳ ✳

OUTDOOR SUMMER CONCERTS

One of the great pleasures of summer in New York is the abundance of outdoor concerts—many of them free to the public.

The Great Lawn in Central Park hosts annual al fresco performances by the Metropolitan Opera and the New York Philharmonic, both of which perform in each of the four outer boroughs as well. Over the years, Simon & Garfunkel, Diana Ross, and Bon Jovi have performed on the Great Lawn to crowds numbering in the tens of thousands.

PROSPECT PARK BANDSHELL

Among the most popular citywide festivals is SummerStage, first held in 1986, which brings more than one hundred free performances in every conceivable genre to parks across the five boroughs each summer. Celebrate Brooklyn! has been presenting an exciting mix of established and emerging performers in Brooklyn's Prospect Park Bandshell since 1979. With Brooklyn's rising profile in the city's cultural landscape, this festival has become a magnet for breakout indie bands.

THE UNION SQUARE GREENMARKET AND CITY STREET FAIRS

Founded in 1976, the first Greenmarket in Union Square consisted of only a few stands. Now, nearly two hundred local farmers, fishermen, and bakers gather to sell their fresh, local produce to eager New Yorkers each Monday, Wednesday, Friday, and Saturday from early morning until the last bunch of lacinato kale is sold.

Warm weather brings a tempting array of culinary treats onto the very streets of New York. You can sample ethnic, multicultural, and a wide variety of warm-weather foods at street fairs in all five boroughs.

LEXINGTON AVENUE STREET FAIR

LADIES
PAVILION

CENTRAL PARK WEDDINGS

Each year, thousands of New Yorkers take advantage of Central Park's many romantic and charming areas, some intimate, others grand, as sites for their fairy tale weddings. Uptown, the Conservatory Garden (actually three gardens in one—French, English, and Italian) is a grand and popular site for ceremonies, while mid-Park, many brides and grooms favor Cherry Hill, with its backdrop of Bow Bridge and Bethesda Terrace. More intimate sites include nearby Wagner Cove, and Cop Cot, a natural wooden gazebo on the crest of a hill near Central Park South.

Here's to the newlyweds!

CENTRAL PARK
BOATHOUSE

CITY BEACHES

One of the wonders of New York City is that you can enjoy the sand and surf without setting foot outside of the city's five boroughs—and when temperatures climb in the summer, New Yorkers in droves do just that.

Orchard Beach, located in the Bronx, was dubbed "the Riviera of New York" when it was developed in the 1930s. The 115-acre site features a 1.1-mile-long boardwalk, two playgrounds, two picnic areas, and a slew of ball courts. Jacob Riis Park, built in 1932, is located on Jamaica Bay in Queens. Its magnificent centerpiece is a historic Art Deco boathouse,

which is listed on the National Register of Historic Places. Brighton Beach, a predominantly Russian neighborhood on Brooklyn's Coney Island Peninsula, boasts beaches that are every bit as beautiful as Coney Island, its more boisterous neighbor to the west.

True to its maritime heritage, Staten Island has several beautiful beaches, none more expansive than the Franklin D. Roosevelt Boardwalk and Beach, a 2.5-mile stretch of Atlantic oceanfront that features a stunning view of the Verrazano-Narrows Bridge.

APOLLO THEATER

HARLEM WEEK

Harlem Week—which actually lasts most of August—brings a dazzling array of concerts, sporting events, food, fashion, and family activities to the brownstone paradise that centers on 125 Street in Manhattan.

ST. NICHOLAS AVE

Renowned venues such as the Apollo Theater vibrate with the sights and sounds of internationally known acts, while the streets themselves come alive with performers from down the street and the world over. Strains of jazz, R & B, reggae, Latin, soca, and gospel music fill the air. Institutions such as the National Jazz Museum in Harlem host concerts, lectures, and symposia. And parks, like St. Nicholas and Marcus Garvey, reverberate with outdoor concerts and events.

Past performers during Harlem Week have included luminaries such as James Brown, Usher, Chaka Khan, Aretha Franklin, Patti LaBelle, Max Roach, Ornette Coleman, and many, many others. Be sure to check this year's schedule!

GOVERNORS ISLAND

An ice-cream cone-shaped green haven in the middle of New York Harbor, Governors Island is a summertime paradise for picnickers, hikers, bicyclists, ballplayers, and art and music lovers—not to mention lovers of plain old leisure. Reachable only by ferry for the precious few summer months, the island hosts art installations and classes, music events, nature and historical walks, and much more throughout the summer.

 WEEKEND GETAWAYS

Anyone who has spent a summer in New York knows that the city empties out on weekends, as locals flock to the area's beaches, mountains, and rural areas for some much-needed rest and relaxation.

The Hamptons, on the south shore of Long Island, are probably the best known of the New York area's weekend destinations, from chic East Hampton to "land's end" at Montauk, which still boasts an active fishing industry and superb surfing. No cars are permitted on nearby Fire Island; life there slows down and you can enjoy the barrier island's beaches and nature preserves in their purest form.

South of the city, the New Jersey Shore, with its fabled boardwalks, music venues, casinos, and popular beaches, beckons.

Many New Yorkers are drawn west of the Hudson to the Catskill Mountain area, with its charming small towns, rustic farms, pristine hiking trails, and waterways.

Within a hundred-mile radius of the city, there's something for everyone!

FIRE ISLAND
FERRY

To my parents,
Gordon and Fran,
who inspire me each day of
every season
with their courage,
grace, love, and strength.

ACKNOWLEDGMENTS

With deepest gratitude to the many people who have helped me make this book a reality.

Firstly, to Jeffrey Keefer for his never-ending support, devotion, and encouragement.

To Sideshow Media for all of their time and guidance in producing this book
and especially to Dan Tucker, who put the words to my images.

To Elynn Cohen for all of her hard work, insight, and diligence on the design.

To my editor and publishers at St. Martin's Press, BJ Berti, Sally Richardson, and Jennifer Enderlin,
for their unfailing excitement and encouragement for my work and ideas.

To my St. Martin's family for constantly keeping me at my best.

Special thanks and gratitude to Janet Erdman, Joellen Church,
the team at Landmark Creations, Joseph Barilla, Mary Ellen Boyd,
Benjamin Bradley, Bruce Wayne, Kristin Chenoweth, Jane Scott, Kristin Franzese,
Marisa Johnson, Lynne Bragonier, Ali Schwartz, Richard Warner, Marcia Rodriguez,
Peter Lloyd, Katherine Suskind, Andrew Mandell, Penny Powell, Tina Worthington,
Barbara Crews, my Christmas friends at the Golden Glow, my sister Donna Parr
and brother Gordon Storrings Jr. and their families, and to the collectors of my work
—your kindness and support are priceless to me.
And last but not least—to my puggies, Posey Pugglesworth and Spencer,
for being such good models and for giving me some good breaks between paintings.

NEW YORK IN FOUR SEASONS

St. Martin's Press books may be purchased for educational, business, or promotional use.
For information on bulk purchases, please contact Macmillan Corporate and Premium Sales
Department at 1-800-221-7945, extension 5442, or write specialmarkets@macmillan.com.
For information, address St. Martin's Press, 175 Fifth Avenue, New York, NY 10010.

www.stmartins.com

Produced by Sideshow Media, New York
Publisher: Dan Tucker
Managing Editor: Megan McFarland
Text by Dan Tucker and Megan McFarland

Library of Congress Cataloging-in-Publication Data Available Upon Request

ISBN: 978-1-250-05101-1

First St. Martin's Press Edition: October 2014
First Limited Edition, The Plaza Hotel: September 2014
10 9 8 7 6 5 4 3 2 1

Printed in China